IN-HOUSE COUNSEL 101

IN-HOUSE COUNSEL 101
SURVIVING AND THRIVING AS IN-HOUSE COUNSEL

Brendan M. Sullivan

© 2022 by Brendan M. Sullivan

All rights reserved. This book or any portion thereof may not be reproduced or used in any manner whatsoever without the express written permission of the publisher except for the use of brief quotations in a book review.

ISBN: 9798830991711

For Dominique. I hit the lottery with you. To my daughters, love you. To my mentors, thank you. To my bosses—both the good and bad—thank you.

CONTENTS

Introduction ix
Part 1: The In-House Counsel 1
What In-House Counsel Is 6
What In-House Counsel Is Not 10
How to Get the Role 14
A Snapshot of a Day in the Life 19
Various Structures of an In-House Legal Department 29
The Pros and Cons of Law-Firm 32
    versus In-House Work
Part 2: Tips and Tricks for the In-House Counsel 37
Day One Advice 37
Art of Meetings 39
Tricks of the Trade 42
    (Difficult Coworkers, Managing Expectations, People-
    Pleasing, Rogue Employees, and Managing Outside Counsel)
Building a Legal Department 51
Negotiation (Deals and Decisions) 56
Adding Value 63
    (Raising Folks Up, Making a Legal Ask, and
    Complicated Concepts)
Restoring Relationships 71

Part 3: Closing Out the In-House Counsel 101: 75
   Maintaining the In-House Counsel Role
Department Dynamics 75
Staying Informed 80
Pro Tips and the GC Gig 81
A Snapshot of the Successful In-House Setup 83

INTRODUCTION

Unlike calls and emails from law firms, this book is going to be short and sweet (yes, shots already fired). This 101 is under one hundred pages. I cannot take credit for all the lessons shared in this book—dozens of mentors and bosses (both good and bad) helped to create this guide to surviving and thriving as in-house counsel. The tips from this book come from almost a decade of working as in-house counsel at Fortune 500 companies, global companies, and start-ups. I think if you implement the tips provided, you should know whether the in-house job is for you. And, if you are already in-house, you should know how to (1) improve coworker interactions, (2) better manage your workload, (3) create and provide solid solutions to typical issues, and (4) renew your sense of purpose in the role.

To set your mind at ease, Excel was not used in the writing of this book. And for the math haters: going forward, there are no charts, no fancy statistics—just page numbers and solid lessons learned from boots on the ground and work in the corporate trenches of in-house experience.

Who am I? In my in-house role, I work with excellent firms, mentors, lawyers, business folks, and executives. I am an in-house generalist, which I'll explain later, and I take a completionist and pragmatic approach to what I do. I've worked with, negotiated against, and spoken to dozens of law-firm lawyers and in-house lawyers. I have negotiated hundreds of deals, hundreds of compliance issues, and hundreds of marketing campaigns and sent five hundred million emails (just kidding on the last one, but it feels like it). I realized across my in-house network, although we all have very similar experiences, we have never put our knowledge in one spot, and a lot of folks are curious about the in-house job. Hence this book.

This book is for the college student thinking about law school and their career options; the lawyer thinking about going in-house; maybe a gift to a friend who recently went in-house; an anonymous gift to your in-house counsel if they're struggling; required reading for a new lawyer on your in-house team; or, if you are already in-house, for those of you who want less headaches. This book is also for the law-firm lawyer who supports a company that does not have in-house counsel but works regularly with various departments within a company.

In predictable legal fashion—and please don't gag, but I have to say it (because some of you love a lawsuit)—the tips in this book worked for me but may not work for you, and in implementing any of them, you do so at your risk. Keep in mind the tips here are not legal guidance regarding the law but merely tips on how to best function in the role of in-house counsel within a company.

Phew, the disclaimers are done, so…there are a few goals for this book. Primarily I want to make the in-house counsel job as sustainable and successful for the reader as possible. By sharing the lessons and solutions that took me a while to gain and how to avoid in-house frictions that my peers and I have hit, the reader may be able to appreciate the in-house counsel role for what it really is. For those who are already in-house, I hope this book serves as some sort of relief or comradery and provides solidarity about the things that you encounter day in and day out and, until now, may have thought were unique or abnormal at your company or in your role.

Secondly I want to demystify the in-house counsel role for future in-house lawyers and make the in-house counsel role more enjoyable and productive for current in-house lawyers.

Lastly, and to be honest from the get-go, a part of writing this book was my selfishness. I want to work with good in-house lawyers. I think this book should be required reading for all in-house lawyers. I have worked with some great lawyers who were just awful in-house counsel, and it made my life harder. Most of the time, they weren't happy with the role either. Whether they were slow perfectionists in fast-moving companies, overly political from bad habits learned at law firms, or unable to work well with the business, those people impacted me and other lawyers and the company's bottom line. Those bad in-house lawyers hurt the legal department's relationship with other departments and added to our workload. Most of those bad in-house lawyers went back to firms or they got better—but they would have gotten better sooner had they read this book. So please require this book if you have or hire in-house lawyers, are thinking about going in-house, or are in-house and it's not working for you.

Here are some of the basics to set the stage:

1. Working or being "in-house" means you are a lawyer employed at a company (rather than a lawyer working at a law firm). You are a part of and support both the internal legal team and the business. Note that when the legal department or in-house counsel refers to the "business," they mean the nonlegal departments within a company. "Legal," or the legal department, is a part of the business, but for this book, think of the nonlegal departments collectively or individually as the business. The business and legal work together to operate a profitable, compliant, risk-balanced company.

2. The in-house counsel job may seem simple or self-explanatory, but trust me, it is a craft and trade. The role takes time to get used to and good at, and in fact, almost every new in-house lawyer fresh from a law firm gets shell-shocked for months or years going in because of the job. Many experienced in-house counsel get burned out at some point, and that burnout can last years. I hope this book paints a realistic picture of the job and, for those in the job, offers a renewed sense of enthusiasm and hope.

3. Not only does the job take time to get used to but even excellent in-house lawyers and solid legal departments can have strained relationships with other departments.

Most often that strain happens when the business is missing their goals or when there are less sophisticated business teams that haven't worked much with in-house counsel / a legal department and don't appreciate the real value of doing so. I believe these strained dynamics can be improved with the tips in this book for the benefit of all and the bottom line. I also know quite a few law-firm lawyers daydream about the in-house gig. I hope this book helps them decide and, if they go in-house, helps them succeed.

So, to close out (and I hope you continue on), this book will get you started on the right foot as an in-house lawyer and help you effectively navigate difficulties in the role or put you back on track to not only surviving but thriving as in-house counsel. Among many topics and tips, the book will get into how to get the in-house job, pros and cons of the role, department dynamics, working with execs, negotiation tips, job security and losing counsel jobs to AI (I doubt that and get into it later), building legal departments, and the general counsel (GC) gig.

The book is three simple parts can be read within an hour or two and save you hours and hours of frustration in the future. For a book the price of one big, fancy coffee, your in-house life should be markedly improved, and, even better, you could be done reading the book before you even finish that coffee.

I hope one takeaway you'll get is to work at a company where in-house counsel and the in-house legal department are seen as a part of the team and as working *with* the team and not *for* the team. With the right understanding of what legal does and the right attitude and recognition from the business, the result is cooperation, mutual respect, and fast, good, profitable work.

A good in-house counsel is an ambassador with and between other departments; a translator of complicated legal terms to groups that either don't care, don't understand, or don't have much time; and a pragmatic triage specialist to help things move forward rather than bottleneck revenue channels and growth opportunities. The relationship between the legal department and other departments is important and should consist of mutual respect for the value they bring and an understanding of pressures on both sides.

A lot of the tips I propose in this book are dismissible as "easier said than done" or something "the business would never go for"; however that is a tad defeatist and, in my experience, untrue. The business is made up of people, and most are more understanding than you'd think. The business wants a high-performing, efficient, responsive, and value-adding in-house counsel and legal team, so if you let them know how to get there, they will flow in that direction.

Breaking the Book Down

Part 1: *The In-House Counsel*
I explain what the role is and is not, how to get in, what legal departments and companies often look like, and the law firm–in-house counsel comparison.

Part 2: Tips and Tricks for the In-House Counsel

I share seven tips centered on making the in-house counsel job the best version it can be with the least amount of friction or frustrations. Tips include how to handle day one; tricks of the trade, like building a legal team and legal process within a company; managing meetings; managing outside counsel; managing other departments' expectations and coworkers gone rogue; deal strategies; adding value, like raising people up in nonlegal departments; junior-to-senior lawyer interactions; and creating or restoring relationships with the business. I also lay out some of the usual legal concepts that confuse nonlegal folks and provide simple ways to explain them.

Part 3: Closing Out the In-House Counsel 101: Maintaining the In-House Counsel Role

This section consists of four parts, ranging from understanding departments' dynamics and working with their people to the corporate county club. It also includes staying informed and raising other people up, pro tips (as a gift for making it through all less-than-one-hundred pages), and a snapshot of a solid in-house counsel / legal department.

Quick Highlights

Here are a few dos and don'ts of in-house counsel that will be broken down throughout the book.

Do:
1. Create as many form contracts and templates as possible and educate the team on using them (starting with an NDA).
2. Create and communicate professional lines and boundaries with the nonlegal departments (the business), including how they can send you requests, how to get one-on-one time, and how long to expect your feedback to take.
3. Create a contract review and legal request policy and have folks sign it so they know how to create proper context for the work, what to send you, and, on average, how long things will take to get back to them.
4. Raise up the nonlegal folks by creating regular trainings (record for new hires) and explaining typical complicated legal sections/concepts in a simple way, including the value-add you bring, how you can work best with them, and what your role is and is not.
5. Stay informed by taking continuing legal education courses (CLEs), subscribing to and reading law-firm blog posts, and reading industry magazines.
6. Stay connected with your legal team by having solid and regular banter via a messaging platform or monthly short check-in meetings for morale purposes.
7. Keep your outside counsel spending down by managing the workload sent to them, holding them to timelines, and working with them to scale back excess.

8. Keep relationships with other departments solid and have an appropriate sense of humor (they need to like to and want to work with you).
9. Bring solutions to all the issues you flag.

Don't:
1. Procrastinate or play politics
2. Overstress
3. Shoot from the hip without getting reasonably informed
4. Get too personal or too robotic (be a professional)
5. Assume (have empathy)

If you enjoyed the book, please keep in mind that my company OneVie LLC offers three valuable products that make your in-house life easier, as listed below. Please email founder. onevie@gmail.com to learn more. I hope you enjoy the book and we can work together someday.

Here are the products available through my company:
1. For nonlegal teams, I offer training on how to structure a deal or campaign.
2. For nonlegal teams, I offer a "demystifying" and "how to work with legal" training (this helps them help you, which helps everyone and the bottom line).
3. For the in-house lawyer, I offer a confidential consulting service to help work through professional in-house role issues with an NDA and an agreement. I can be a sounding board to you on your in-house journey

Brendan M. Sullivan

(limited to professional guidance on the role and not specific legal guidance on a legal matter).

As the French say, *on y va*! Enjoy and good luck! Let's get you not only surviving but thriving as in-house counsel.

PART 1:
THE IN-HOUSE COUNSEL

"What do you do again?" This is a question that I get all the time from my friends, family, and even folks that I work with outside of legal. I often say, "I do commercial deals." I used to hesitate to say I'm in-house counsel for a company because people either didn't understand or they don't like lawyers, and I didn't want to be hit with ten lawyer jokes and a middle finger. What I've never said but should is that I review ads, draft and negotiate contracts, create terms and conditions, review compliance rules and regulations, settle disputes, try to lower law firms' bills, strategize with various departments on profit and risk, and read and send dozens of emails a day. I feel like I would lose my audience with that. Nowadays, I do say I work at a company as their lawyer and "do contracts and stuff." Sounds boring, but it's not, and I love it.

Understanding what the in-house counsel role is (and is not) is critical because it will help drive the decision to take the job, stay in the job, and do well in the job. The in-house counsel job truly is a craft and a trade. Convincing nonlawyers to think of the big picture and potential what-ifs when their mind is focused solely on deadlines and commissions is no easy feat. Negotiating with an opposing lawyer who has decades more experience or digs their feet in on a nonissue because they personally just don't want to do the deal is painful but possible. I've seen quite a few law-firm lawyers come in, hate the in-house job, and happily (and quickly) leave. I've seen some nonlawyers visibly shocked when they realize in-house counsel can and do have a sense of humor and are not all like the divorce lawyer who destroyed them or like their last robotic in-house counsel who took days to respond and almost always said no.

This chapter is broken into five sections: what in-house counsel is, what it is not, how to get the role, a snapshot of a day in the life, and how to structure a legal department.

I knew I wanted to go in-house before going to law school. In college I sat in on a trade law presentation by an in-house lawyer at a global company, and his job sounded awesome and dynamic. I like making deals. I've been making deals since I was eight. I never wanted to work at a law firm. I enjoy working with sales folks, finance people, and marketing gurus. I like finding solutions and getting creative to make things work. The in-house job has allowed me all of that.

In my opinion the ideal structure within legal is flat reporting—there are bosses to approve time and run ideas by (who have more experience or have been there longer), but in general, the lawyers work together to support the business. I like hybrid-structured legal departments (some generalists and some specialists) unless there is a true need for specialists (because of unique employment or product or service issues), but even then, the specialist should have a generalist, customer-oriented mindset and understand the overall business. I think it is important for a company to treat legal as part of the business, a respected support function that adds value and is never seen as a cost center nor as a control function or the check box / principal's office.

As mentioned, I am an in-house generalist. There are also in-house specialists. I get into that breakdown in the "Structuring Legal Departments" section of the book. Some law-firm lawyers dream of the in-house gig and the end of tracking hours, working with toxic partners, and client butt kissing. Sorry to burst bubbles—and don't get me wrong, I love the in-house job—but the law-firm lawyer dream and reality of the in-house role are not the same. The in-house role is dynamic: internal departments need you almost every business hour of every day; the issues that pop up are often absurd and allow very little time to vet or think about; and for most in-house lawyers, even on big legal teams, you are basically jogging or running from the minute you get in until you get out if you want to keep up.

Keep in mind that a company typically brings in an in-house counsel and creates a legal department for a few reasons:

1. Outside counsel is too expensive or slow (most common).
2. They can now afford a dedicated legal resource, understand the value of in-house, and want someone dedicated

only to their questions and needs who can really get to know their business (rare but the best option).
3. They're growing fast and think they should have one at this point.
4. Their customers are curious about why they don't.

The reasons above matter when it comes to how the legal department is viewed and treated but do not matter when it comes to what you need to do on day one and every day you are the in-house counsel. Your role is to add value by being prepared and informed, be responsive (acknowledge receipt), act and decide ethically, be open minded and listen, understand the business and its people, know the standard forms and applicable laws, be professional, provide solutions, and be comfortable being uncomfortable and standing up and speaking in the company's best interest. Whether your boss or the execs value your approach isn't as important as your reputation and your law license. People are watching and may move to another company and tap you later. Adding value and being a proper in-house lawyer helps with networking and helps the next attorney coming in—if you don't do a bad job, they won't walk into preconceived notions and difficult, resentful, and suspicious business folks. If you can look in the mirror and think, I earned my paycheck and did the best I could given my mental and physical state—good.

Understanding what the role is and what it is not is important to communicate to nonlegal folks as well. Even now when I make a joke, some folks don't laugh because legal often has this overly serious reputation that makes us harder to approach. You can change that vibe.

Many departments and professionals have never worked directly with a legal department or in-house counsel before, so when this happens, you have the awesome and important opportunity to be a great first example; raise them up to work smoothly with us, and remind them cooperation and communication are key. This book will really push the business-legal dynamic with many tips and tricks and things to avoid or reiterate each day. If you do your job right, the business won't groan when the in-house counsel needs to be brought in but will have brought you in from the beginning because they know the value you add.

Don't forget: as in-house counsel, it is OK not to know something. We are human and not robots, so if you don't know, just let folks know you'll find out and get back to them—then actually get back to them. Talking in circles to hide your lack of knowledge—or worse, guessing and shooting from the hip—will cause you problems sooner than you think.

Also remember the in-house counsel gig is a marathon, not a sprint. You will burn out if your first and foremost goal is people-pleasing, responding at all hours every day, or constantly accommodating turnaround times that are nearly impossible. Balance is key. Setting expectations with nonlegal coworkers is critical.

The in-house counsel role is dynamic. If you want to work with lawyers and nonlawyers on specific product, service, and business issues and have little control over what you do each day but enjoy the challenge, you'll like the gig. If you're hoping the in-house role is a reprieve from law-firm life or some sort of career salvation, it's not—it's different than a law firm, for sure, but it's got its stresses and difficulties as well—so get into it for the right reasons.

So, with that, let's get into the details of the in-house counsel role and life. If you can make sure your peers, boss, and other departments are on board with what your workplace's in-house counsel is and isn't and does and doesn't do, your life will be easier, or at least clearer.

After you understand what in-house counsel is and isn't, we can discuss how you get in.

What In-House Counsel Is

The in-house counsel is an attorney for a company and typically works in the legal department. Some companies station legal within a specific department like finance or risk. Sometimes a department will have a dedicated lawyer, but usually that lawyer is still part of the legal department.

As you learned, or will learn, in law school, the in-house counsel's obligations and duties are to the company and not to a particular person or department. Although job security does require that people like you enough to work with you, there needs to be an ethical and compliant balance between saying yes to make or keep work friends, what the law actually says, and saying no. A good in-house counsel is able to craft guidance so that they are still likeable while also providing the guidance that is in the best interest of the company—which is usually to inform the business to avoid illegal, unlawful, unethical, and unreasonably risky or unsafe decisions or actions.

The in-house counsel supports the company and various people and departments; however, there is a distinction between working with and working for. The in-house counsel works for the company and typically works with (not for) multiple departments and persons. In my opinion the only person the in-house counsel works for, as far as an individual, is their direct boss. The rest, including an exec or CEO, the in-house counsel supports as long as it is in the best interest of the company. As mentioned, the departments and people outside of the legal department are often referred to by legal as "the business."

In-house counsel is in a high-visibility role. They are needed by multiple departments and dozens of people regarding a high volume of diverse issues, contracts, and matters, so the in-house counsel needs to be available to support.

An in-house counsel does the best they can with the time and facts that they have to come up with a workable solution for the business; they must be pragmatic and almost constantly shifting.

An in-house counsel is usually resource limited. Most in-house counsel do not have junior staff (associates) to research issues or draft for them and do not have a paralegal to make copies. Most do not have access to the best legal databases. Why? They're working for a company; the company can allocate some funding for legal, but it is not a law firm and has to limit how much it can spend on the department. The goal is to get as much resources needed to do a reasonable job.

An in-house counsel is approachable—whether they want to be or not. Any level of employee from any department can come to them with questions; there is rarely any vetting or hierarchy.

An in-house counsel is dynamic. Almost every day is like a law school hypothetical, except it is not a hypo. The in-house counsel needs to figure out as much as they can and then find a path forward—whether they have much knowledge on the area or not. If time permits, company policy allows, and it is necessary, a specialist may be brought in, but for the most part, the company's expectation is bringing an in-house counsel in will reduce the company's overall legal costs.

Reducing costs means the in-house counsel handles as much legal work in-house as they can in exchange for their salary rather than outsourcing to a specialist unless absolutely necessary. The in-house counsel is also expected to carefully and professionally review issues to reduce short- and long-term exposures (money lost or money to be paid out via lawsuits, regulators, customer loss, or vendor issues).

That said, an in-house counsel is also a cost manager and diagnostician. An in-house lawyer will need to know when something needs to go to an expert if an issue is complicated or out of their experience. If something does need to be sent to a specialist, an in-house lawyer needs to manage that cost.

The in-house counsel is expected to meet the expectations

of the role, get to know the business well (and better than a law firm would or could), and help the business be successful.

An in-house lawyer is not always a specialist but is always a generalist. Some companies have a tax, environmental, or employment law specialist, but even then, those lawyers have to step out of their comfort zone and support the business on things that don't fit nicely into their wheelhouse.

An in-house counsel is expected to be able to communicate to nonlawyers in an effective way since that is who they work with.

An in-house counsel is expected to structure and engineer deals—to understand the who, what, where, when, and how to create a work product the business can use within the timeline the business needs.

An in-house counsel is patient. Nonlawyers sometimes don't understand that things take reasonable time, aren't as prepared as they should be, or don't understand the importance of setting the scene or answering the lawyers questions. Nonlawyers may have less deal or corporate experience, a weaker work ethic, less focus, or less ethical training. An in-house counsel is patient and helps nonlawyers help themselves. Other lawyers on the in-house counsel's team may be perfectionists, sloppy, unresponsive, or overly eager, and a good in-house lawyer will try to raise that person up or not replicate that behavior. Learning to work well as a legal team to support the business is key.

An in-house counsel is professional. Respect in both directions, from legal to the business and back, is key. In-house counsel should not be bullied or pressured to give bad advice, burned out, or mistreated. The in-house lawyer should be decisive when asked for their opinion, be able to stay in their lane or shift between them, and be prepared. The in-house counsel should hold the line on proper legal guidance and solid ethical practices and should find a balance at work—or find somewhere else to work. Although customer oriented, the in-house counsel also understands the importance of customer management and creates fair boundaries.

What In-House Counsel Is Not

An in-house counsel is typically not a decision maker for the company or business. The business, with guidance and support from legal and its in-house counsel, will make decisions. Options ranging from where to sell or service to what to sell or offer, what price to charge, who to partner with, employee issues, campaigns, settling a lawsuit or filing one, new markets, new products, and customer or vendor issues—all of these are hopefully presented to legal so legal can give a range of options and potential consequences of certain decisions. Then, the business decides.

The in-house counsel doesn't write or make the laws that apply to the business, nor does it make the decision on how the law will be applied or what a jury will decide. "It depends" is a frustrating answer from in-house counsel to the business; however, most answers to business questions are simply dependent. The in-house counsel needs to then explain what the answer depends on.

The in-house counsel doesn't usually bill departments, have clients, or track hours. The in-house counsel has internal customers, which are various departments, and external customers, like major company vendors. Customers may be just as pleasant or difficult as clients were at a firm.

As aforementioned, in-house counsel is in a high-visibility role, usually requiring normal business hours with a high-volume tempo throughout the day. In-house counsel typically does not get and wouldn't take long lunches and often works through lunch. An in-house counsel cannot typically come in late or leave early. Why? The in-house counsel's customer is the business and its employees. Those employees work normal business hours, never too early or late, and they expect their support function—legal—to be relatively available. Plus, these customers have the facts in-house counsel needs to do their job. Working very early or late at a law firm may work, but when you need to work with others, you need to be working when they are working. Most companies work on multiple time zones, and issues pop up all day that need quick responses. It is hard for an in-house lawyer to play schedule games.

With that said, remember that an in-house counsel is not a robot. They have families, friends, and commitments outside of work. In-house counsel, unlike a robot, does not know everything off the top of their head. Further, an in-house counsel is not a babysitter—or a butler. We'll get into this more later.

All in-house counsel are also not the same; a lawyer is not necessarily going to create a similar bad experience that someone had in the past in working with another lawyer, and it needs to be made clear that each in-house counsel should be given a chance.

In-house counsel is typically not as lucrative as a law-firm gig. At a firm, more hours often mean more money, but not in-house. I do think quality of life can be as good or as bad at a firm as within a company; it really depends on the company and firm. Job security can be similar in both as well. The big paychecks for in-house really come in the form of discounted stock, profit sharing, or getting into a VP or higher role, which is rare.

In-house counsel is almost never the bottleneck it is often accused of being. Fix that reputation early on if you sense or hear it. Sometimes and rarely is legal the bottleneck—that happens when someone in legal is a perfectionist, posturer, or procrastinator; fix that. More likely, though, are complicated deals. Explain how and why the deal is complicated to the business teams. Perhaps there are difficult and slow counterparties, or the business itself is sloppy and messy and can't make decisions or structure a deal for the life of them, and that makes it hard for you to help. Using the tips below, it is possible.

In-house counsel should not be viewed as a cost center; if you're catching issues, making good deals, avoiding big losses, and controlling costs, then you're bringing money into the company.

In-house counsel is not an easy job. It takes skill to get nonlawyers to pay attention, to take advice, to convince or persuade or support teams that become resistant and sometimes hostile if they don't like what they hear. In-house counsel is not a slide-into-retirement-post-law-firm-life-type gig. It is, to me, a fun job and a craft and trade, but it is not easy.

As you'll see later, there are some clear confusions with legal and nonlegal departments, which is why I get into what legal is and is not. That confusion often causes frustration. As mentioned, legal doesn't usually make decisions. Legal's primary job is to inform the business on a decision, not make a decision. We can help and should help by structuring options through decision trees (*if this, then that* and *if that, then this*). We can be a sounding board for execs, and we can list out the consequences and opportunities of a decision, but at the end of the day, execs and nonlegal folks decide. Often business folks don't understand that and look to legal to take the burden of their decision making—that confusion needs to be resolved because it can put you in a tough spot, unless you've been given executive sign-off to make a decision.

An in-house counsel at a small and private company or at a big or public company will not have too much of a difference in the role's definition. There are typically more resources and trainings at a public company and other lawyers to bounce ideas off. Politics, people-pleasing, and posturing exists within all types of companies. A small company may expect you to wear more hats than you thought and work faster, while at a bigger company, you may be expected to hold the line or image of the legal team and stay in your lane as far as legal guidance.

With the above being said, do you want to add value working with lawyers and nonlawyers on business matters? Take phone calls, handle loads of emails, and be relatively uncomfortable with new and different daily asks? If so, read on. Do you want to specialize, take your time producing perfect work, not be asked about areas of law you don't know, rarely be on the phone, and have a set day mapped out? Maybe stay at a law firm.

How to Get In-House

If what an in-house lawyer is and is not and does and does not do is something that you're still interested in, below are three ways for those not already in-house to get into the role:

1. ***Straight in.*** This is rare. I went straight from law school to in-house. How? I worked at a law firm while in law school, had a business degree and international experience, and got my foot in the door doing contract analysis and vendor management work before I passed the bar. Small start-ups that can't afford a three- or four-year law firm associate typically will take a risk and bring in someone with less experience as in-house counsel. Network, use LinkedIn, understand the job description, and sell yourself. This was not easy, and thankfully I had the resources of some great outside law firm partners, legal database software, and the personality to roll up my sleeves and figure it out.

2. **Secondment.** This is less rare. When a firm wants to offer its client a dedicated resource or a firm's associate isn't going to make it in law-firm life or has expressed interest in going in-house, the law firm and client can sit that lawyer in-house for a bit. This is a good chance for the company to get to know the lawyer and the lawyer to get to understand what in-house life is like. From there, if the client really likes the lawyer, they might take that lawyer on full time. Alternatively, in a few months or years, that lawyer starts applying directly to companies. The benefit for firms of placing their attorneys on secondment is theoretically that the lawyer will then outsource work to that law firm.

3. *Networking, Recruiters, and Direct Application.* This method is the most common path to in-house. While working at a law firm, someone wanting to go in-house should establish good relationships with clients. Eventually they would be approached by the client to come work for them. Sometimes the attorney's friend or peer will go in-house and bring them in. The attorney can bring in a recruiter, or a recruiter will reach out to them. Lastly, the attorney can just apply to jobs that sound interesting.

In my opinion a few years at a law firm is helpful on the drafting front and to make an in-house counsel appreciate the pros of the in-house life. A fair number of in-house lawyers and some companies hiring do expect, want, and feel more comfortable and confident when an in-house lawyer has been at a firm for a little bit. Some roles in-house, especially specialist setups in litigation or regulatory law, do benefit from a person with a few years or more spent at a law firm.

That said, most senior lawyers admit that outside of relationships they made at law firms to get expert help and some resilience they gained, their law-firm training did little to nothing in preparing for or making them successful in the in-house role. A lot is gained in the in-house role by learning from experience, CLEs, senior lawyers, and outside counsel. For most, being at a firm first burned them out and made them appreciate the in-house role a bit more. I'd offer caution against hiring lawyers in-house who have too many years at a law firm or hiring teams looking for set number of years for candidates; make sure they're not looking for a workhorse punching bag.

Some Tips for Getting the Role

If you want to go in-house, LinkedIn is key to getting you there. Make a good LinkedIn profile, and search for terms like "in-house counsel," "counsel," and "legal and risk." Check out the Association of Corporate Counsel (ACC). Check out GoInhouse.com. Look into the top ten legal recruitment companies and drop your résumé on their website—even reach out to some of their staff on LinkedIn. Use LinkedIn to see if some of your law school classmates landed somewhere that is hiring. For you to get the job, your résumé should read similarly to the job posting and highlight skills like being responsive, dynamic, a multitasker, etc.

Before accepting an in-house gig, really make sure you jibe with the legal team and the department heads with whom you'll be working. If someone seems like they will end up bullying, harassing, or dismissing you, dig deeper. See what other lawyers think, or wait to work somewhere else, because if that person has power within the company, your work life will be miserable as you constantly try to accommodate, delicately handle, and bite your tongue because of a toxic person.

Before taking the job, also consider whether that company really needs in-house lawyers or should be using a law firm. How to tell? Ask what law firms the company uses, for how long they've used the firms, and whether the company is happy with them. If they've used a firm for a long time or since the company's inception, that law firm has power and mystique and will be trusted over you, and you'll be stuck using them (some techniques on that below). If the executives don't trust legal's judgement or are constantly asking if their preferred firm has also looked at it, if they don't have too many contracts coming in, or if you're viewed as an afterthought, check the box.

If you go to a company that really doesn't want a compliance culture or legal to be a part of the team on the front end—a.k.a. bring in a profit, put sales over everything, and treat anyone else as a punching bag—then you will be left in the dark a lot, you will be second-guessed, you will be viewed as a cost center, and you will have to constantly justify your actions. Sometimes a company doesn't need in-house counsel but likes the idea of it, sometimes a company is going through the growth phase and should have one but doesntbut it's not ready for it and doesn't understand the role— so in those situations when you accept the gig then it isvery important for you to show the value of an in-house counsel or you won't last long. Try to get a sense of the way legal is viewed by executives and by other departments and the relationships it has with other departments before taking a job as in-house counsel at a certain company. Figure out how long the current legal teammates have been there. Make sure the type of company and work is a match for you.

If You Are Offered the Gig, What about the Package?
When it comes to the package to go in-house or take another role, see if there is potential for upward momentum. Really think about what pay works for you. The grass is not too much greener somewhere else—whatever you do now, it'll likely be with similar people and similar work somewhere else, so how much will you accept to make that change and be happy with it? The amount of vacation days is huge; you'll need them. I still usually check my emails on most of my days off, but the ability to be off is key. Try to negotiate in some guaranteed severance. See if they'll pay for bar dues, how much the bonus is, and how much they'll bump pay up within a set number of many years if you are doing well. The package does matter, as does who you'll be working with. My thoughts on this are: find good pay, with good people, doing good deals, and the rest should be golden.

What Does the In-House Counsel's Day Look Like, and What Do Legal Departments Look Like?

In-house counsel who manage their calendars and track their projects have a less chaotic life than those lawyers who do not. There is less posturing and "fake it until you make it" attitude if you're disciplined about what you're working on and keep notes about where you left off and who you're talking to when about what. So that is a pro tip to start. The reason I share it from the get-go is that as in-house counsel, whether you're a generalist or specialist, you'll likely get dozens if not hundreds of emails a day, you'll have things for at least a half dozen departments, and you'll have some projects that are new and some that are over a year old. Organization is key to managing that mayhem.

As Far as the Day to Day

Here's a snapshot of a day with a caveat.

The caveat: The snapshot below is assuming you are at a company that actually needs its legal department (is busy and not outsourcing to law firms constantly), that hasn't hired too many lawyers, and that is doing well on the profit side of things.

The day: At a company similar to the one mentioned above, most days are super busy; from logging in to logging out, you're in meetings, answering emails, or working. Think at least eight- to twelve-hour days (working through lunch) four out of five days of the week. Expect this workload and level of intensity for 75 percent of your year. The usual expectation is that you're available when the business is there and needs you. Even at very busy companies, the business is typically not working on the weekend, so unless you're really backed up, you wouldn't be working either. Some days are reasonable, where you can get to what you planned—about 15 percent of the time, you're managing well and not running full speed. Ten percent of the time, you'll have a slow go of it, and that is really nice; you can catch up with CLEs, get emails organized, do company trainings, etc. So many absurd things come up all day, every day, it often starts to feel like a law school hypo and not real life—but if you're creative and a problem solver, a wrench in the system should get your craft, skills, and energy going to figure it out. If random, crazy things popping up would bother you and you want a consistent and predictable day, in-house may not be for you.

On the communications front: you could expect about three to five meetings a day, and often people try to squeeze in more meetings last minute. You'll get anywhere from thirty to upward of two hundred emails a day. You'll also be called and messaged on platforms like Slack, Teams, and others. Remember, I started this section with "stay organized."

On the work front: you'll almost always be on a quest to find the signed document that you need to review or a good form to use, and sometimes you need to make forms from scratch. There are a whole bunch of contract management platforms, but if people aren't uploading them, it's a bit of a grind. Expect to be working in no less than two or three different databases each day. Your boss and execs will be dropping requests on you randomly each day or week; you'll want to find out how urgent they are and likely prioritize as you report to them.

And with the volume mentioned above, you've got to add value to the business the entire time. So let's get into that.

Adding Value

Although the business may think "adding value" means accepting whatever deal they've given you and just saying yes, that is not adding value and will get you and them in trouble. They or their boss or the execs hired you for a reason, and it was likely not to be a *yes* person. That does not mean you should be a *no* person. You need to add value by doing your job.

Adding value to the business is critical. The business pays your salary. Adding value means different things depending on whether you're a specialist or generalist, but what adding value means almost universally in-house is that you help the business make better (faster, smarter, more profitable) decisions (including resolving issues that could spiral) and avoid bad (costly, unmanageable, profitless, lawsuit-likely) decisions.

Adding value is knowing the business and its short- and long-term needs. Adding value is knowing what you do, staying aware of the industry you're in, and being responsive, supportive, and professional each day—in short, justifying the paycheck you agreed to. We dig deeper into this in the section regarding tips and tricks in part 2 of the book.

Closing Out with the Realities of the Role

In my experience and in talking with dozens of in-house counsels, the common stance is we don't have much control over our days. We have to-do lists, but they're often thrown out the window before nine o'clock in the morning because things just pop up all day. That is what can make the job stressful, chaotic, and frustrating or exciting, depending on how often this happens and your ability to triage.

As I mentioned, in-house counsel can expect a lot of emails, phone calls, and meetings. Some get more emails than others, but nowadays, most folks prefer to email. When emails aren't getting you the answers you need, you should request a call. As far as calls go, a lot more video calls—and a lot more calls in general—are happening in this new remote world. Remember, meeting after meeting from 8:00 a.m. to 6:00 p.m. means you're not getting any time to work, eat, or use the bathroom. It is not sustainable. That is mismanagement of time. You need to vet which meetings you accept, think about hiring more folks, etc. The art of meetings is explained in part 2.

Before a call with a third party, an in-house lawyer should make sure they're not on calls that a third party is on but doesn't have legal counsel on, should reduce the number of calls where there isn't a clear ask or needed legal support, and should be on the calls where there are legal questions.

Emails can be frustrating. People miss questions, badly answer them, send half-written responses, don't explain requests or questions, and often fabricate timelines that are unrealistic and not urgent. The business often forgets to attach a document or sends one without context or a clear ask. This is an opportunity to teach the teams how to best email with counsel. On the note of responding to dozens or hundreds of emails, let people know what to expect. I typically will respond within the day that I receive it. I use a contract review policy for them to understand the timeline for me to review/edit once I have what I need. I will let people know that I will not immediately respond to a message or email, but if it is urgent, they can mark it so, put time on my calendar, or try to give me a call. On the note of urgent—I do make sure they understand what "urgent" means (urgent to them or urgent to the customer versus urgent to the company) and coach them whenever they miss the mark. I try to remind the business that we have all to be reasonable. The legal department supports many people and departments. If it takes that person three or four days or sometimes weeks to respond to my email, I should get at least a few hours.

The in-house lawyer can also expect absurd deadlines (which in hindsight are humorous but in the middle of chaos, suck). We get into it more in detail later, but wishful or selfish thinking seems to rule the day with the business when it comes to deadlines, at least until better controls and processes, mature conversations, and mutual respect work out, with you leading that effort. Even then you'll get someone asking, "Can you look at this by EOD and let me know if we're ready for signature?" at 4:30 p.m. with twenty-eight pages of redlines. Sometimes there really is an urgency. That being said, people not doing anything until their boss pings them or right before they leave for vacation—that is a teammate problem, not a counsel problem, although it can create a legal problem. This is an opportunity for education and observation. Explaining why things take time to review and the importance of getting it to you early with context (the who, what, where, when, why, and what they think and need) always helps. Let people know your average turnaround time (with proper context and documents) for you to send back edits or questions. At the very least, acknowledge you've received the document and counter-propose a time that works reasonably for you to do it. Observe who are the last-minute fire drillers—they can create legal risk, so definitely try to help them improve if there is a pattern; if not, time to get supervisors involved.

The in-house lawyer will still typically need to speak with outside counsel. The calls range from thirty minutes to one hour. There are tips and tricks below to help you manage outside counsel. The reason you need outside counsel even when you're in-house includes things like really niche areas of law, complicated projects, how much volume you have, and litigation.

The in-house counsel quite often will work on research or a contract for hours, weeks, and sometimes months, and a decision is made to quit that deal or project. That can be frustrating, especially if it was touted as urgent at the start. Just remember, that work may get picked back up, and you get paid either way.

The in-house counsel will need to speak with the "other

side," whether a third-party customer, vendor, opposing counsel, or regulator. Being prepared and understanding the business's goal should govern what style of negotiation or tone you take.

In-house counsel will also need to take CLEs and company trainings. These can take up a good bit of time, and HR does care if you've done them. It's not great to be the compliance-minded group that fails to comply with internal training policies.

Working with Your Boss as In-House Counsel: The Good and Bad

The in-house counsel's boss expects a few things: First, that you can reasonably do the job. A good boss understands that people are difficult, but if you are given what you need to do the job, you can do it. Second, that you will be responsive and deliver on timelines or communicate when you need more time and why. Third, that you keep relationships with other departments solid and do not participate in or cause drama or friction if you can avoid it, and if you can't, you push back professionally to not damage legal relationship with other departments. Fourth, that you manage outside counsel spend. Fifth, that you make reasonable decisions, and they can trust you. Lastly, that you escalate big issues reasonably so they are not caught off guard by something you're working on.

You can and should expect a few things from your boss, like political protection by assuming you are not the problem, an innocent-until-proven-guilty approach, not allowing other groups to disparage your department without speaking up, not micromanaging (you were hired to do the job, so let you do it), support when resources are needed, responding when escalating issues, and keeping you informed of company happenings at the higher level. If you're doing your job well, you should expect flexibility on time off, pay bumps, and genuine accolades. Your boss should also not sit on projects; a bad boss (even if busy) agrees to a timeline, sits on the issue, and then gives it to you last minute. Work with your boss to not have that happen again by stressing it could hurt the department—that sitting on issues is some law-firm passive-aggressive or sloppy procrastinating habit that needs to be ironed out, or people will be unhappy in that legal department. Sometimes things fall through the cracks, but this should be very, very rare because of proper organization or because someone else had it fall through the cracks and you're asked to step up. Expect your boss to get you the time you need or to protect you from a short review time and not to make it a pattern.

In part 3 I discuss maintaining the in-house role and understanding others. That is key for the day-to-day friction or day-to-day success.

Bad bosses do exist for in-house counsel. You'd think they'd be so grateful to be out of a law firm and have had the time to become a solid manager and keep the toxic stuff out of the legal department. But truthfully, some people just aren't meant to manage other humans. Either because of insecurities, trust issues, power goals, toxicity, vanity, ego, or personality disorders, some bosses can just be brutal. A good relationship with a boss is key, but that relationship should be based on mutual and earned respect. No boss is king, even if they have a lot of power within the company.

A good boss, when they see you add value, is grateful and enables and advances you, while a bad boss sees you as a threat. A good boss will try to make you look good and not bad. A good boss will put your job security ahead of their own. A good boss will send you decent work and not the work they're themselves afraid to touch or with people they don't like to work with. You'll know a bad boss when you see one. Do your best with a bad boss and try to find a dynamic that works—or, if that boss has a lot of power and isn't going anywhere, then start looking for a new job. You can learn how to not be with a bad boss, and that is a value-add.

Even with a boss who is a "good lawyer," that can mean a lot of different things: a good drafter, a good negotiator, a person with an encyclopedic knowledge of the law, or a problem solver—but none of that means a "good lawyer" will be a good in-house lawyer or a good manager. So for those of you dismissing bad treatment from a boss or about to hire a good lawyer but bad person, be careful.

If you do not want to manage other people, don't. If you take on management and hate it, trust me, it is going to suck for you and everyone under you if you aren't committed to putting your personal issues aside and learning to do it well. So here's a tip: if you see a revolving door of lawyers under a few senior lawyers who have been there for a long time, it's almost guaranteed you've got a bad-boss situation or an execs-who-don't-value-legal situation—either way, not good. If your job security depends on it, and the only time your boss is decent to you is when and if you allow them to mistreat you without guilting them, appease and compliment them, take blame for them, and hang out with them after work, enjoying the same jokes, hobbies, and music as them, then you need to get that résumé spruced up. Turnover is really expensive, and constantly changing lawyers is bad for the business, so for execs and soon-to-be-in-house lawyers who will someday make general counsel, don't be a toxic person. People have families, and karma does come around. There are a lot of mirrors in office buildings, restaurants, and homes—you can't avoid all of them.

In my experience, though, most in-house bosses are fantastic, and a lot can be learned from and through them. It is nice to become friends with who you work with, and it often happens, but it shouldn't be a requirement; a bad boss is a sad person, and you can do better. Life is easier when people respect and want to work with and for you. Low morale is fixable, but a powerful bad boss is often not.

Tips on the bad boss situation: (1) anonymously send them this book; (2) remember, it is just a matter of time before you find something else, but while you're there, do not let them jeopardize your reputation or law license; and (3) stay calm—it is them, not you, and you'll be OK in the long run.

Lastly, in-house counsel can expect executive interactions. Keep emails and meetings/answers short, sweet, and concise and come with recommended paths to issues. Be on time, be ready to answer, and do not talk in circles. If you don't know, admit it and state that you'll find out. Then find out and close the ask.

Structuring Legal Departments

Legal departments are made up of at least one counsel and sometimes support staff like a paralegal or contract manager, and the counsels are generalists, specialists, or both.

A generalist is decent at, or can learn to become decent at, any area of law or can learn to find affordable, competent specialists to outsource to if and when they can't get up to speed on that area of law. In short, the business can go to a generalist with any legal ask and get some sort of support / game plan. A generalist can become uncomfortable or overwhelmed with too many varying asks.

A specialist has a niche area, like environmental law or employment law, that the business only goes to for that issue. A specialist can become bored with that area of law or overwhelmed with the number of asks.

Some companies have one and some have up to eighty or more in-house counsels. The titles and department structures are typically as follows, regardless of size.

Titles:
- Counsel (one to six years of legal experience)
- Senior counsel (six to twenty years of legal experience)

- Assistant general counsel (ten to twenty-plus years of legal experience)
- Deputy general counsel (ten to twenty-plus years of legal experience)
- General counsel (ten to twenty-plus years of legal experience)

The biggest difference in roles is largely the general counsel. This person not only manages the legal department but also is a major support function and almost an on-call staff member for executives.

Structures

There are various structures. Some companies have a bunch of specialists, and the business knows who they are and goes to them. Some companies have lawyers support various regions of the country, and some companies have a hybrid of the two. To break it down:

1. *Regional legal support structures.* This setup includes counsels that exclusively support different regions of the country or globe and all the potential legal needs in that region. The pros here are really getting to know the nonlawyers in various departments based on region and getting almost to the specialist level on regional issues. The cons of regional setup include more need for outside counsel; some regions are busier or slower than others, which isn't fair for that lawyer or other lawyers

in busy regions or slow regions; and some teammates in certain regions are just tough to work with, and because of where you live, you as the in-house counsel are stuck. Regional legal support typically relies on a generalist in-house counsel rather than a specialist.
2. *Specialized legal departments.* Various counsels offer niche areas of legal guidance to all employees. For example, everyone at the company might go to the employment lawyer about employment-law issues. The pro here is having some up-to-date knowledge on the laws in that area and not as much need for outside counsel. The con is that bottlenecks can get created as specialists get backlogged. It is often a hard role to fill because specialists would often make more at a law firm.
3. *Hybrid legal departments.* These departments offer national support. In this structure you'll see both specialists and some generalists, and projects are divided by the type of work, service, product, and sometimes region. This is my favorite setup. There are similar pros and cons as the above.

In terms of structure, at some companies, a few departments report to and are under the legal department. I think it makes sense to have compliance, risk, insurance, and sometimes finance departments reporting to and under legal. I do not think the HR department should report to legal; I think it can cause problems. I do believe legal should support and make sure the HR department has power—even power over most execs on the process of hiring and firing, which will allow for a really solid, ethical company. HR needs the power to get rid of bad eggs, even bad eggs high up, rainmakers, or bad eggs within the legal department. Otherwise the company is constantly at risk of morale issues, turnover, and/or bad and unethical decisions caused by repeat and serial offenders who don't get fired because HR reps aren't listened to or they fear for their own job security if they were to try to advocate what is right for the company. Legal can help convince execs to give HR more power on holding the line for decent, competent people in the company. Legal and HR should work together to create policies; establish processes for risk and legal compliance on warning, hiring, and firing decisions; and create a safe and ethical workplace—but HR, in my mind, should be separate from the legal department.

A legal department in a small or private company rather than at a big or public company can be, and often is, set up similar to any of the variations above, although it is rare to see a specialized-only department. Note that in part 2, I discuss how to create a legal culture and legal team.

As to the Pros and Cons of Law-Firm versus In-House Counsel Work

Here is what I've gathered from law-firm folks who turn down in-house gigs; law-firm folks who went in-house, then back to a firm; and law-firm folks who went in-house and are glad they did.

Law Firm Pros

Firms allow you to become a specialist. Being a specialist can be great because you can become known for that niche among many customers. Law firms are more flexible about what you do with your time as long as you hit your billables (long lunches, late days, early days, long nights). Law firms allow you to work mostly with lawyers, which means educated, usually informed and prepared, competent, and responsive folks (for the most part) who have ethics and licensing rules that lead to a certain expected behavior threshold. Law firms typically provide more resources, including paralegals, clerks, and junior associates. Law firms offer the flexibility of lots of different issues and customers and unique things to handle day in and day out. Law firms can compensate well as you move up the ranks. If you're hitting billables and doing a good job, your job is secure. People are held accountable; if you don't hit billables or are bumping heads with customers or coworkers, that gets fixed sooner rather than later. Even though your guidance is expensive, most customers are grateful for it.

Law Firm Cons

You have to hit your billables. Senior attorneys with power can make your life hell. Your customers are often trying to cut down the bill. You have to handle all customers with white gloves because it is important to make money. Hours can be insane. As you progress, you often become more of a client manager than a practicing lawyer, schmoozing with customers and managing frustrating junior lawyers. You may not have control over when an ask comes in and lose a weekend or night and miss important life events. Job security depends on you being responsive to the customer. You likely have to wear a suit, button-down shirt, tie, and/or formal shoes..

In-House Counsel Pros
You have more control over your calendar, and it's very rare to lose weekends or have long nights. There are no billables. You do have to be respectful of departments, but you don't have to provide white-glove service. HR departments (except at family-owned or very small private companies) don't typically allow too much nonsense from senior folks, so there is an element of respect. Working with the business can be refreshing, and you can step into a legal-business hybrid role. You can move from legal to other departments. It is interesting work, and you can see the results of your work. You typically don't wear a suit, button-down shirt, tie, and/or formal shoes.

In-House Counsel Cons
You don't know what you'll be working on. You often don't have much time to do anything and have to get comfortable with risk. Expect tons of emails daily. When you take a vacation, the work just waits until you're back. You probably won't make as much as you would at a firm (although you often have good insurance, a 401(k) / retirement account, and, for some, profit sharing and/or stock discounts). Job security isn't as good as it

is at firm because it isn't based on how good a job you're doing, but how well you're liked and how the company is doing financially. I know a lot of in-house lawyers who have been at quite a few companies, while I only know a few law-firm lawyers who have been at more than three law firms. Some of the people you work with in the business aren't vetted well and simply aren't great at their jobs or nice to others—and there isn't much that is done about it. Even if you give great guidance, a fair number of business folks aren't grateful for your guidance because they would have preferred not to go to you at all. It's one of those things: people feel better if they pay more for a firm and are often more patient with the firm; we're harder on family than friends sometimes.

Tip: If you enjoy the in-house counsel role and do well, you can move up the ranks. I've found this is done the fastest by switching companies. Outside law firms that you work well with may sometimes give you tips on which of their clients are looking to hire. Other in-house counsels step into legal/compliance, risk, or strategy gigs; start their own; or go back to a firm. In-house counsels often end up as CEO, CCO, COO, operations leads, and finance/strategy leads—except for the general counsel role, those more business-oriented positions do tend to pay more. The experience itself is worth it.

PART 2:
TIPS AND TRICKS FOR THE IN-HOUSE COUNSEL

The tips and tricks below should help get you started and keep you successful as an in-house counsel. After the tips I provide some examples of issues that could pop up in the role and how to navigate them.

Day One as In-House Counsel

On your first day as in-house, I highly recommend the following:
- Get all the form contracts you'll need or that the company has. Read them and get to know them.
- Ask for a solid contact and decent person from each department.
- Figure out which law firms the company currently uses, for how long, and why (Did your boss use to work there? Are they family or friends of the owners?).
- Create folders in your inbox to stay organized. As new deals come in, create new folders and move the emails

into them. I like having an Excel cheat sheet of major projects, who the business lead is, what outside counsel may be involved, and the general latest status.
- Block out a few minutes or hours every week for you that can't be moved for meetings.
- Ask your boss for all the compliance manuals, forms, risk tolerances and thresholds, trainings they've given to the business, and any weird quirks the company has, from subsidiary management to logging issues, etc.
- Meet with your boss to understand what is important at the company on appearances versus performance. What I mean is, does your boss or the execs monitor who comes in and leaves at what time? I call those folks "clock watchers." I find them interesting because while they're watching others, they're not working. I think they feel less anxious and more comfortable knowing people are in early and leave late, as if it is proof they're getting what they paid for. I try to steer clear of that. First and foremost, just get your job done reasonably well and in a timely manner. Be generally available for the business during business hours when they'll need you. Let people know if you're going to be on vacation in advance and have a backup lawyer or tie things up before you go—that prevents a lot of panic. As far as hours, those people coming in at 7:00 a.m. and leaving at 7:00 p.m. might only actually work a few hours and spend the rest reading the news. It's a bad and toxic gauge

of working. In my opinion (your boss's may differ), be there during normal business hours with reasonable flexibility, don't miss meetings, don't take three-hour lunches, and don't make a daily pattern of bouncing early and arriving late. If the business feels supported, your deals are getting done, and you're working about as much or (probably more often than not) more than your agreement requires, your boss should be fair. You've got an advanced degree, you're an adult, and you know what you're doing. Yet if appearances are important, until that culture changes, do your best to comply, and lay on thick how much (how long) you're working.

The Art of Meetings

- I'm a huge fan of letting the business know that the best way to catch me and get my full attention is to put time on my calendar; I explain it avoids phone tag but also allows me to prepare and know what the call is about. I recommend you take this path as well. Keep in mind that the business, even if told to make sure you're not already booked during a certain time gap, won't. Don't be frustrated; just get comfortable declining those overlapping meetings and providing an alternative time, letting the meeting requestor know why you're declining and offering a new time. You can also decline and not propose a new time—instead, just

- list out better times for you.
- Whether a one-on-one with your boss or an internal customer, always give as many days advance notice as possible for a meeting.
- Keep meetings as short as possible to get the info you need or explain what you need to explain. If more time is needed, you can always find more time later in the day or week. For meeting invites, always attach the document you'll discuss in the meeting; also list out a few bullet points about what will be discussed and the goal for the call.
- Create meeting rules for other departments that want you on a call. Let them know advance notice is appreciated so you can prepare for the call, tell them you can't join if the third party doesn't have counsel on the line, and advise that each meeting needs to have materials attached, context, and goals prior to the meeting—or you might reject it because your assumption is there is no legal ask and you were added by mistake.
- If there are back-to-back meetings and meetings drafting on too long, start having teams advise what can be done via email, ask to start the call with the legal asks first, and if needed, ask them to list priority deals and start saying no if it isn't urgent or priority and can be discussed later.
- If someone is constantly talking in circles, bullying, or speaking over others in your meeting, interrupt and just

state that you appreciate their feedback and that you can get on the line to dig deeper, but you've got to get through a few more points, and you'll let them know when it is their point. Truly there are serial interrupters; make sure you direct the meeting like the ambassador you are. Some people act badly in meetings as a tactic to avoid progress, some are just annoying, and others just aren't self-aware.

- Have meeting etiquette. Do not be late for meetings, and don't let others be late either.
- If you have back-to-back meetings: Things happen, so if you think a meeting is going over and you have one following it, then let everyone know there are X minutes left and then you will drop, and they can schedule more time if needed. Alternatively, let the next meeting know you'll be five minutes late—before that meeting starts—and apologize. It's better to just not be late.
- If others are late: After five minutes, if it is a key person, message them and state that in five minutes, you're recommending the call end, and that person can propose a new time. If it's an exec, offer to propose a new time, but let them know that the call will end. If someone is late, but not critical, and says they're sorry for being late, let them know someone on their team can send a recap, or you can if they need it, but you're going to keep pushing forward. Recommend a meeting etiquette policy. If someone knows they're often late or will definitely be

late, have them put a representative on the call to take notes. If they're a decision maker who needs to be on the call, simply require they be on it or propose times they can make a call on time. Recaps during the call put everyone over, take time, and are not fair to the people who are on time. That being said, reasonable and one-off exceptions are understandable—just recap quickly. As calls are getting close to an end, even if everyone offers to stay on, it is my recommendation that a new time is proposed so people can use the restroom, check emails, and not feel pressure to stay on.

Tricks of the Trade (Difficult Coworkers, Managing Expectations, People-Pleasing, and Rogue Employees)

No matter where you work, difficult coworkers exist. Finger-pointing and the blame game—this happens everywhere, but it happens a lot more to in-house counsel because your customer is departments with people of varying skillsets, ages, and preferences who have their own pressures and deliverables. A less sophisticated business (one that hasn't worked often with legal before) or a badly performing department often (and usually unjustly) see in-house counsel as being in the way of their goals and the cause of their delays. In-house counsel is, in short, just an easy target for nonperforming, overly demanding, or procrastinating departments or individuals and is usually too professional to play dirty and too ethical to lie.

If the business is sophisticated and healthy, they see legal as a value-add and bring them in early. If they are not, they scapegoat. A smart and sophisticated executive team or leader knows the truth, and it's not a hard case to prove the problem wasn't the legal department, but showing that someone is difficult isn't adding value. Adding value is finding a way to work with that difficult person and get things done. Please keep in mind that in rare cases, legal is to blame either because they're slow (perfectionists or overworked), or they failed to communicate how long it would take to do something and why.

If you can figure out why a department or person is being difficult, great…but it's unlikely.

So first, try to avoid working with difficult people or departments altogether by being on the right foot with the business when you start working there. Let them know you are there to help them help themselves and get things done as quickly as possible, and let them know the way to do that is to give you as much advance notice as possible, keep you in the loop, give context, and answer your questions fully to reduce delays. If they prefer phone calls over emails, do it. If you've been there awhile, it is never too late to try the above tactic.

If the business has selective amnesia or is playing the blame game, just let them know you always follow up calls with an email recapping. And do so. If toxicity, blame and/or unresponsiveness go too far, be direct and ask them whether you did something and how you can help them better—but also let them know there is a base level of respect that needs to be had, and you need their cooperation in finding a dynamic that will work. If you still can't get them in line, talk to your boss, talk to their boss, talk to HR, or, as a last resort, start looking elsewhere if the company is OK with this type of person. Most people pointing the finger are the problem, and they're a problem for lots of other people, too, so as long as you're documenting your work and guidance, don't get too stressed—other folks see the value you bring. After each call with difficult people, they may hate it, but email the group or the person you chatted with and document what was said on the call, what they'll do, and what you'll do. This documentation is great to have down the road. In the worst-case scenario, if the difficult person is entrenched and powerful, your boss should protect you and just have that person go to and through them—or if it's bad enough, start looking for another job.

If on your first day and every day while you're the in-house counsel, you're clear you really want to help the business make good deals in an effective and inefficient way by helping them help themselves, the list of difficult people will drop because it will become obvious to many other people that you're not the issue—they are, and they'll lose that scarlet letter *L* (legal) to blame for their inability.

Truly some business folks just hate and will never get along with a lawyer. If you can figure out why and show them you're not what they hate, great. Often, though, they've had bad experiences with past in-house counsel, they wish they were a lawyer, they resent your personality, they assume you make a ton, or they've had a bad lawyer interaction in their private life—whatever it may be, some just can't let it go, but they do need to cooperate enough to get deals done. If they don't, raise it with your boss, HR, and their boss. That being said, sometimes it is you. If it is you, figure out what you can do to work with them better, and truly try.

I can tell you most things aren't urgent. Someone either sat on a deal, their boss asked them about it and they haven't done anything, they're about to leave for vacation, or it's escalated to the point they need to act, and their created problem sometimes can become your problem. Debrief on that and meet with their bosses and yours if it becomes a pattern. Most people within the business are great; it really is a small group of repeat offenders who make the day hard. If you can solve them, you're golden. If you can't, you'll still be OK; it's just a matter of them leaving or you leaving, and at least they are consistent and predictable with their shenanigans.

On managing expectations, the contract review policy is great. That tells them that you need at least X amount of time to review. I like three to five business days from my receipt of their package (and often do it sooner). Three to five days is useful because the business often forgets the in-house lawyer is not just the lawyer for one department or one person but probably a dozen-plus people and a half dozen departments, so if everyone is asking for something, we need time.

Another key to managing expectations through team education is to let the business know what it is you actually do and why it takes time. If it's a campaign, each policy/statute matters; if it's a deal, each section matters, and the short- and long-term risks need to be considered. More often than not, we don't overthink, but we do think, and that does take context and time. If they know the high level of what we do when we get a contract and receive some education on what certain sections mean, the business is usually more patient with their in-house lawyer.

On the note of an unresponsive department or person, keep this in mind: Don't take it personally, and don't assume they're being difficult. Execs are busy, everyone is getting too many emails, and a lot of business folks just simply don't have the time or desire to read or write emails. Figure out who is who, and for those who just suck at responding electronically—call them. If you need their feedback, find a way to get it; if you truly can't, ask your boss or their boss who else might know the answer. Make sure everyone knows that things get done faster the sooner legal can get the response it needs.

I also consider bad responses to be an issue. If you're asking three questions and only getting two answers or you're asking a few questions and only getting one-word or unhelpful answers, schedule a call, walk them through it, and reiterate on the phone and in the email that you want to help them get it done, but you need more info to do so. I give the "I hurt" analogy in the adding value section below.

On the people-pleasing front, of course it matters if people like working with you when you work at a company. It makes it easier when both sides want to cooperate and can tolerate meetings and emails from one another. Some people are in their role purely because they're liked by someone in the "corporate country club" or powerful folks. That's fine, but also be decent at your job because there is a lot of anxiety and insecurity for those folks with job security that depends on whether they're liked and no one figuring out they don't do much. In people-pleasing there is a difference between being likable and going beyond your ethical and legal obligations as the in-house counsel representing the company with an oath with the state bar. You may really like a coworker and want to support them or really want a coworker to like you; in the alternative, you may really want a coworker not to dislike you—but you have to do your job well and treat people fairly. Even a powerful department or person cannot do whatever they want unless they own the company. Your job is not to do what you're told by one person or one department; it is to provide internal legal services in line with the best interests of the company, the law, your bar obligations, and your job description. Sometimes in people-pleasing those you're providing services to, you can forget that you often do not work for them and can go too far. Make sure you balance support and reasonable accommodation with ethical and legal standards for the job.

Risks are created within a company when people in other departments don't know what is going on. If I think someone has gone rogue on a project or deal or is offering something we don't or can't do or haven't vetted then I will put a call together with that person and other departments. The goal of that call is to gain consent and cooperation from other departments on the issues and to try to get that person or department where they need to be with a focus on the company's time and money. Legal has a line of sight on deals that not every department has, and we have the responsibility of keeping the whole company coordinated when and if we can. Other departments should do the same for us. In my experience most sophisticated companies have departments that never keep other departments in the dark about things a department should or may need to know, and that makes things faster. Bottlenecks truly do get created when someone goes rogue and doesn't have the buy-in or feedback from other groups. Ready, fire, aim is a dangerous thing. Raise people up to get ready, aim, then fire, and your company will quickly start hitting more targets with less friction and wasted time, money, and energy.

Managing Outside Counsel

This can be tricky. Often when you get into a legal department, the lawyers already have a firm they routinely use. That can be good because that firm knows the business and its people well but can be bad if the firm overcharges or is slow. If a company doesn't have a firm picked out, it may be up to you to choose, and that can be tricky because if they take too long or are too expensive, your boss or the executives might blame you.

So, what to do?

- If the firm commonly used by your company is slow or expensive and you're asked by your boss to find someone better priced and faster or your own sanity demands it, talk to your boss and start with a request that is gentle (in case there are friendships involved or that person picked the firm). "Hey, X firm is great, but they're getting backlogged with some issues / I've noticed they don't have specialists. May I vet other firms—like a mini request for proposals (RFP)—to see if they can do smaller tasks faster and cheaper? Is that OK?" Typically you'll get a green light.

- Run the work scope by a few firms and ask how long it would take or what their total time or cost estimates would be. Make clear that you don't want a long memo or multiple associates or partners. Go with whichever firm seems the most excited and has the relevant experience to do the job within the parameters you want. Ask them to keep you in the loop on timing because the business will want to know the status of the request.
- When the bill comes, make sure it reflects calls that were actually had. There are often mistakes, and it's uncomfortable but not unprofessional to fix those mistakes; plus, your boss or the business may want the bill explained.
- I typically like when the department requesting a need that requires a specialist helps pay the legal bills so that the legal department's budget doesn't get crushed. That means you can't be outsourcing everything because things will slow down too much for the business, cost

too much, and—well, why are you there if you're outsourcing all the work?
- Once you get guidance from outside counsel, share it with the rest of the legal department and, if you're sharing it with nonlegal folks, make sure you explain it in a shorter version. You have to pay attention to the guidance you're getting, and remember, even if you've outsourced it, your boss and the business will want to know the request's status and have you translate the complicated law-firm guidance into practical business advice. Take notes, be on the calls, and read the emails and the memos. Outsourcing to a law firm does not remove your accountability and responsibility on the project.
- Whenever you're doing calls with outside counsel, have an agenda and keep things moving. They are artists at making calls take the full hour, but as in-house counsel, you're busy, so if it can be done faster, ask them to do so.
- Whenever you're including the business on a call or email with outside counsel, let everyone know that any additional asks for outside counsel need to first be scoped internally by the legal department / in-house counsel and that before the firm gets started on something different or new, they should wait for your approval. Also make sure that you are cc'd on any of the firm's emails with the business and that it knows it cannot start legal work without someone from the legal department approving

that work. Outside counsel spending can get crazy if the business just starts going directly to outside counsel, and technically you are the representative of the business, so outside counsel should—but doesn't always—know better. Plus, there may be past precedent before you got there that may cause them to think the business can work directly with them.

Building a Legal Department and Team

If you're the first in-house lawyer or have the opportunity to build or rework a legal team and department, here are some tips.

Building and Growing the Legal Team
- First, when you're bringing in candidates, make sure all in-house candidates interview with and fit with the department heads that they'll be working with from a personality perspective and experience perspective. That means people should be honest during interviews about how they like to interact, what their style is, and what they need help with.
- Make sure all candidates jibe with the executive expectations and culture of the legal department; be honest and self-aware about what that is before interviewing the candidate.
- All in-house candidates should interview with other lawyers and staff on legal. Allow the current lawyers and

staff to interview the candidate as well. Advise people to be honest during interviews.
- Before hiring someone, paint a clear picture to the candidate of what day one, week one, month three, average days, and a few outliers will look like, and make sure they seem to genuinely desire that reality.
- Be careful with too little or too much law-firm experience. What does the legal department need, what does the business need, and can this candidate get there relatively quickly? Will they be shell-shocked or not?
- Don't hire too many lawyers without a clear and long-term need. Be honest about temporary high volume and demand, and understand if there is a business slowdown, the execs might see the cost of legal as too high.

Creating a Legal Department Culture within the Legal Team and Across the Company

- There is the external image, spirit, and culture the legal department has with other departments. Think about what you want this external image to be and how to get there. For me, I want the business to view the legal department as decent people who are responsive, informed, caring, and respected; add value, and are never viewed as bottlenecks, robots, butlers, or servants.
- There is the internal image, spirit, and culture the legal department has within itself among lawyers and legal staff. Think about what you want this internal image

to be and how to get there. Why would someone want to be on this legal team? For me, I'd want to make sure lawyers and staff can bounce ideas off each other and care about one another, sharing ideas, tips, and stories. Handling difficult projects requires people in lockstep—a united front. This can be done through group calls, group chats, or emails. Not being alienated or siloed from other lawyers is great. We can get busy and focused on the tasks, but stepping out and catching up with the other lawyers is critical to the marathon of the in-house life. Do serious work in as light as possible a manner. Ensure the team has the resources they need to perform, responses to questions or issues, protection and an innocent-until-proven-guilty attitude from their boss, and training. In short, the legal team should be confident and comfortable in their job and job security.

- Be cost conscious but creative. Your lawyers need to stay sharp, and paying for bar dues, providing reasonable access to resources they need to do their job, and having an outside counsel budget is very important for morale and bandwidth, but don't get too fancy. The business and executives often forget how much you save them from avoided or settled disputes and the money you gain them from well-created deals and initiatives; they simply see your monthly cost to the company, and everything needs to be justified. Don't get stingy, but don't get too posh in spending money on and for legal. I find that it's best to make the department that has a specific legal need that will require an expert the one to budget for that outside counsel fee, and it's our job to pick the firm, get a reasonable estimate from the firm, hold the firm to it, and make sure the department requesting it understands on the front end the time and cost it will be charged. If legal has the burden of all outside counsel fees, it can be problematic if the company is tight financially and layoffs happen or it's salary-increase / bonus time and the company is already uncomfortable with legal costs. It's always great to have documentation to show how much was saved and gained by having the legal department.

Creating a Legal Culture throughout the Company

A legal culture is one where the nonlegal departments understand the value that internal lawyers bring. Examples of legal's value include catching deal killers in the beginning of a negotiation and offering solutions to make those killers workable to negotiating important terms that were missing, motivating a customer or vendor to do the right thing, settling disputes before they become lawsuits, controlling outside counsel spending, handling marketing and compliance issues, and helping to grow and scale the company by amplifying profits and reducing unreasonable risks. Often a healthy legal culture is a top-down situation. If the execs are on board with legal being a part of the business team, sitting at the table from the get-go, and listening to, cooperating with and scheming with legal, the rest of the company will as well. A healthy legal culture is one where the business knows the rules, there are clear policies in place, they are enforced, and the business knows what to bring to the lawyers, how, and when. Deals and projects will get done faster if legal is seen as a teammate, brought in from beginning to block and tackle deals, and viewed as important internal advisors and supporters but not butlers, or check-the-box or control functions.

If you can help the execs and business understand the importance of giving you enough time to review by explaining what goes into review, making sure they get you signed documents and draft documents in a form you need, and that they read and pay attention during legal calls / compliance checks, you're well on your way to an easier day. To do this, I recommend creating a contract review policy, compliance policy, and document retention policy, then recording the short context of what these policies are and why they're important. For a contract review policy, make sure you include the time it will usually take legal to review provided legal is given all it needs (and list those needs out in the policy). Make sure communication and trust exists. Legal is not trying to get the business in trouble or paint them into a corner—we need to know what's going on so we can help. Have them call or set meetings if there are questions or gaps they're concerned about.

A lot of the pushback and frustration with legal is simply that the business doesn't know what goes into negotiating a deal—why it's complicated and takes time. Explain it quickly to them. If they understand what you're doing, they will be a little timelier on the front end but faster, more cost effective, and more profitable in the long run, and you'll be golden. Time may kill a deal, but a very bad deal may kill a company.

Negotiations: Deals, Pace, and Decision Issues

When the business comes to you with a deal, provided they gave you the who, what, where, and how of the deal, you should also find out how important this deal is to them, their department, and the company in general. Why? If it is a critical deal and you are a critical attorney, you might be lighter on the redlines if it is the other side's form, or you might be more flexible with the submitted information on your company's form. Further, the approach you take if and when you get on the phone with the other side may be that of a bulldog, a peacemaker and facilitator, or a car salesman—all smiles and handshakes. That is another thing to find out: What is the approach the business wants you to take? Is this a difficult counterparty they're tired of? Did we piss them off in the past and really need to "Gandhi" (make peace) with this legal team and company? These are all good things to know.

I like to get on a call with the internal asking department to learn more background about the counterparty and deal before even redlining. Before having a call with the other side, I also like to have a prep call internally to see how they want to handle the call with the other side and what approach I should take.

The other side's in-house attorney will likely do the same. In my mind and in the minds of the dozens of other awesome lawyers in-house with whom I've worked, a win-lose style isn't great. Deals take longer, and you have a bitter counterparty before business has even begun. Win-lose leaves one side irritated and almost always leads to problems, terminated contracts, or lawsuits. A win-win or win-tie is great. Have things in your pocket to give the other side, flag the issues that are critical to your team that have to be pushed harder on, and offer solutions for both sides so no one gets stuck, and both sides will appreciate you. If you have a difficult lawyer on the other side, you might be able to have your business lead talk to their business lead about getting their lawyer to be more reasonable—it works. If the deal really is important and desired on both sides, the business can help motivate legal to unstick themselves. That being said, sometimes we get stuck on legit issues; find out when you start from your boss or the execs what things you absolutely shouldn't make exceptions for and hold to them. If an exception is to be made, capture that decision by the exec to make the exception in writing (email) in case it comes up later.

On the deal front, I really don't like to be the lawyer for the other side, meaning they pitch me an idea and ask me to "take the pen." I usually push back on that with the justification that I don't want to guess at what exactly they want, as I might miss and waste time on repeat, so if they can send me the paragraph or sentence they want—or even better, just redline the document and send it back—I can take a look.

Deal Process

Also, before even redlining or reviewing the other side's redlines, I highly recommend you have the requestor confirm a few things:

- Did they look at the edits/document, and does it line up with their goals and discussions? They have with an eye toward business terms like timing, obligations, pricing, et cetera. If they say no, have them do so because often they've sent an older or wrong document, and it's better for them to realize then before you waste time. An ideal and sophisticated business will know to take a look before sending a document to legal.
- Ask them what is in there that they want out or isn't in there that they want in. And as mentioned before, make sure to get the context (who, what, where, when, how, and why).

On drafting and negotiation (and handling absurd deadlines):

- Ask them about deal timing—when do we need to review by, and when does it need to be signed by? If they say it is urgent (to them, yes, usually, but to the company, rarely), but it's a lot of work, ask for justification and make sure they're aware that if you prioritize this, their peers' deals will be pushed aside and you'll have to let the other teams know. If they're still claiming it's urgent, let them know how much time you realistically need based on the amount of redlines or pages. If they still need it on a time crunch, remind them of the contract review policy, and let their boss know you'd like to debrief because of course urgencies happen, but they are rare, and if someone sat on this, that is an issue. Then in your review, put in writing you did not have time to fully vet the documents and that the review was done in less-than-ideal time. Recommend again that more time be given in the future to mitigate risk.

- Map out main issues or which sections, if the company get stuck with them, could cause certain risks to the company.
- Do the best you can with the time you have (or don't have). Often I like to ask the business to give me three to five business days from my receipt of everything I need and lay that out in a contract review policy; I often do it sooner, but it's nice to let them know they need to get ahead of things. I will also ask them to be fair and give me as much time as they have had it in their inbox, the time the other side got to review or respond to it, or at the very least those three to five days.
- When listing out issues you've flagged, give a high-level overview in the email; under that, give bullet points, and then flag it in the margins of the attached. Get the business to comment within the document, or have a call, then document in email what the business is willing to accept.

Slow Deals

When it comes to slow deals, legal is often accused of being the bottleneck and blamed. It is easy to blame legal, but really—what's the word?—basic and, by doing so, never gets to the heart or pattern of the issue, and so it repeats.

In my almost ten years' experience of claims of slow deals, it is hardly ever the legal team that keeps contracts from getting drafted, negotiated, and signed quickly.

When it is the legal team bottlenecking deals—again, very rare—it is because of the following:

- Either a perfectionist lawyer, a posturer or procrastinator afraid to get in the mud and get started, or an incompetent lawyer—those reasons are pretty obvious pretty quickly. Individuals who cause these issues need to be dealt with because they hurt the reputation of the whole legal team and hurt the bottom line of the company.
- Too much legal work with outside counsel, which can slow things down. In that situation, get your company some form agreements, stop customizing deals, or get better staffed outside law firms.
- A legal team that just isn't big enough for the deal volume. When that is the case, the lawyers there need to triage and do the best they can with the time they have, prioritize certain deals, communicate this issue to the business, outsource more to outside counsel, hold outside counsel to a set deadline, and try to get a new lawyer hired if that volume will continue for at

least three months or more. Sometimes secondment is a quick option. This situation can become unsustainable for the legal team, and people may quit; it can also really frustrate other departments, so if this is the bottleneck, take a half day to figure it out.

Most of the time, the reason for slow deals is actually the business being slow. One thing they're really bad at is reading and fully answering emails. If you can really stress to the business that although they are not lawyers, they can and need to read and know the basics of the deal and respond to the emails with the context of having read the whole email to help speed things up for them, things will go fast.

Often deals go slow because there really isn't a deal yet. The business and the counterparty don't really know what they want to do exactly yet; they're excited and something is coming, but there aren't specifics, and legal can't draft hypotheticals into a concrete contract. So this delay is due to a premature ask.

Sometimes the business knows what it wants to do but wants to use the other side's form, and it's very one-sided—that means a ton of redlines. Sometimes it takes the other side a long time to respond to redline requests. Sometimes the other side really redlines up your form agreements. Sometimes redlines require business feedback and decisions, and the business just doesn't respond or know what to do. But it is not legal's call to decide deal points that will impact other departments, so without feedback, in-house counsel can't draft. Then from there it's a matter or waiting on other departments for their feedback, waiting on the other side for their feedback, and then the issue of who can sign what. I recommend a job title relative to the value of the contract to determine who can sign what. A strategically structured deal plus cooperation and communication can get deals done quicker, but for in-house counsel, it is often like pulling teeth from all the nonlawyers who claim they want a deal done but don't show up to meetings or provide timely feedback. In these situations, be sure to document all the calls you've made asking for responses/feedback and all the proposals you've made that have gone nowhere, and at the end of the day, communicate what it will take to get the deal done and who you need what from so that it can. I recommend having a deal lead on the business side who takes responsibility for pushing deals through because at the end of the day, it's their deal; we just inform and support it, and it's only our deal until the contract is signed (and partially after if there are questions). A deal lead with a project manager can really help the lawyer get what they need to speed up deals.

Decisions

Decisions issues can be a real problem for the in-house counsel. From who can sign which contracts to what timing or structure the business can live with or what redlines or deviating terms the business can accept, all require multiple department head approvals/feedback. Again, a project manager and deal lead are critical, and the in-house counsel can and should lay out via comments in the margins and bullet points who and what department needs to review what, why it matters, and what you think might work. Even after all that is done, though, it is sometimes very hard to get someone to decide yes or no or propose something else. Why? Job security, procrastination, morale, motivation. That is an executive issue. The best thing in-house counsel can do when there is decision fatigue, decision resistance, and decision gaps is to inform the business what legal thinks; remind them without the decision, the contract or deal can't be finalized; and document this via email. It's always helpful to offer a call and recap what decisions may have been made when.

Adding Value

We discussed this briefly earlier in the book in the day-to-day section. If you take that and add the tips above, from working out bottlenecks to keeping legal costs down, you're adding value. Another way to add value is to avoid a lot of the issues above simply by educating nonlegal staff and managing their expectations. If you can raise up the nonlegal departments on how to best work with in-house counsel, if you can make it so they bring you in early and are glad to do so, and if you can get to the point that their reaction to learning in-house is getting involved isn't to groan but to breathe a sigh of relief, good. If you can explain in a short and clear way why certain things are important—like NDAs or indemnity sections (i.e., we owe them or they owe us money and have to pay without a court requiring it)—the smoother both of your days will be because more knowledge means less frustration. For every issue you identify and flag, offer various solutions.

I like to start training my legal folks like this: We want to help you, and we want things to move smoothly, so picture this. You walk into the doctor's office and simply say, "I hurt," but you don't say where, how long, or what the pain level is. The doctor asks. You don't respond, or you give unhelpful or uncooperative answers. Chances are you're either going to get the doctor saying, "I can't help you," or a bad diagnosis. Walk in, be specific, give him your medication history, and cooperate—he's going to get you squared away. Sometimes that means more testing; sometimes this means medication right then and there, and sometimes it means seeing a specialist. That is how the in-house counsel works. We can't guess; we need to know more than just "I hurt." Legal is a part of the team; it does not work *for* the team, but it works *with* the team.

Adding value is key for job security, so on that note, I wanted to address the discussion about in-house counsel jobs and law-firm lawyers being replaced by artificial intelligence, robots, and automation. Some people in the business think this would be great. That is sad because they don't see the value in in-house counsel or have had bad experiences. They also aren't aware of why that wouldn't be great. Here are my thoughts on why this won't happen soon or entirely.

On the pro side: Automation and AI are great for the in-house lawyer to pull cases, proper forms, etc. The tech doesn't require health insurance, doesn't show up late, and doesn't quit.

On the con side: The technology isn't there yet. The cost of the tech will increase as it replaces lawyers. The tech won't cover a lot of the needs of the business.

Most companies want to customize deals and forms specific to a particular customer—I don't see a day when everyone is using nonnegotiable forms. If the forms are negotiable, risk and opportunity is created, and a lawyer will be needed because it is a new concept. Further, there are always operations issues, customer service issues, and new laws and regulations no one has analyzed yet, so there will likely always be a need for someone to do the thinking and assess how to navigate the what-ifs of real and hypothetical proposals (which the business loves).

To help legal add value, it is great for the nonlegal team to understand a few things from the start about the legal department and in-house counsel:

- First and foremost, things aren't usually complicated, but they do require some thought, time, and cooperation from the business, so if legal asks for context or questions, answer them.
- Legal can inform decisions but does not usually make decisions. We can make a decision tree for the business showing who the decision maker is, and we can lay out pros and cons, but usually the business needs to tell legal what it is going to do once informed.

- Legal is not usually a bottleneck or slow. Things do take time, and often, if the business doesn't give us enough to do our job, our license and ethical obligations require we wait until we've got what we need. Plus the other side can be slow, and sometimes the deal just isn't at the drafting stage or the issue isn't at the decision stage.
- I try to teach that the contract is like the bible for our business. Whatever it says—someone has to do X by Y time at Z price and all the details—then that is what we must do. We may not look at the contract for weeks, years, or ever, but we need to know what our forms require—or what is required of us—and we need to honor it because if an issue pops up, all parties go back to what the bible (contract) says.

Again, a clear issue is when the business doesn't know how legal adds value. Let them know legal adds value by creating better deals. It can help them make better informed decisions, which means more money in and less money out. Legal can spot and reduce unreasonable risks in an effective way and increase short- and long-term opportunities to profit by thinking strategically about what can and can't be done because of their knowledge of the law, contracts, and the business. We can save time and money if we're brought in early and listened to. We want to make the other departments look better and do better because our salary depends on their bringing in money and not losing too much of it.

First and foremost, as mentioned before, many in the business have never worked with in-house counsel or the legal department before. Let them know your style of doing business, how to get things done fastest with you, and what you do and don't prefer. See what they do and don't prefer, and let them know things will move faster if your emails are read and answered fully, if solid levels of context are given in legal asks, and if you're brought in early so you can spot and recommend solutions before the situations get too far along. Try to get the business to understand that if it's a document that requires a signature and can require the company to do something, legal should know about it and advise on it. Just getting them to understand what to bring you and when is a huge value-add for both of you.

Some Things to Help the Business Work with You

- ***Teach them how to make a legal ask.*** First, when presenting a legal ask to you, the business should provide context—in other words, scope or structure—of the deal in the ask/email and give you the who, what, where, when, why, and how. If they don't know the deal, or the ask is premature and shouldn't be coming to legal yet, they should ask you what you think about it. Things like timing, costs, and commitments are all for them to tell you. The better they can structure a deal, the better you can draft it, and the faster it will get signed.

- ***Provide a contract review policy.*** Outside of structuring a deal is the contract review process. Make sure they know what types of projects, deals, marketing messaging, or contracts need to go to you (as mentioned above, if it binds the company or requires a signature, it probably needs to come to you), how to get it to you, what to provide with it when they send it to you (see above regarding context), and how long it will typically take once you have all that you need.
- ***Raise them up by getting them more sophisticated on the legal front.*** Another way to raise them up is to make sure they all understand basic legal concepts that matter to that company and explain some typical contract terms that often end up getting sticky and why it matters that we work them out. Often when the business knows what is happening behind the scenes and why what is decided in the contract matters, they're more appreciative and helpful and less skeptical of or frustrated by legal. This explaining should be done like a nonlawyer in a business-friendly, short, and simple way. In short, help them help you, which helps everyone. Below are a few concepts that I've found that confuse or frustrate the business and how I've explained them:
  - An NDA: It's not complicated; it can be short and sweet, and it is critical *before* discussions about confidential concepts happen. Ideally a mutual NDA allows both sides to speak. Only share what is ab-

solutely necessary. I also let them know they look better when they propose an NDA and it gets signed because it signals two things: (1) this is a real chat with real potential benefits, and (2) the person they're talking to is sophisticated enough to know what an NDA is and that it is important. Teach them how to make an NDA request: They should send the NDA they want reviewed (or ask for an NDA) and always tell us what the conversation will be about (what we are sharing with them and they with us) and with whom (the actual entity name and address, if possible).

- Other things like RFPs need to be read by the business to see if we're even interested and then what the consequences are for bailing. Get them to come to legal early to flag areas another department should decide or that should be redlined or commented on before the proposal is submitted.
- The below contract sections can be better explained as follows:
  - An indemnity section can confuse nonlegal folks. Basically it's a contractual obligation outlining that one side has to pay the other side back for certain set things. It matters if there is no limit to what should be paid back, and this request can and should be done outside a court order.
  - Another section that confuses nonlegal folks is

termination and term—how long the contract is and how easy it can be gotten out of. It matters because, a lot of the time, money or noncancellable orders can be made, and there can be certain damages if someone jumps ship earlier than expected.
- Nonsolicitation and noncompete sections are hard to manage. Poaching is just a bad game and a downward spiral, but these sections need to be reviewed carefully and closely, and HR should be informed.
- Choice of law also matters because some states don't have business-friendly laws. If the other side is founded in and hires a lot of people in that state, that can make neutral or objective, fair decisions more complicated.
- As for breach of contract and remedies—basically if we say we're going to do something in the contract, then we have to do it; if we don't, and we don't fix that failure within an agreed-upon timeline, we could be sued for damages. The contract matters, so if we really don't know about timing or a certain representation, then we shouldn't say it.

The business often doesn't understand what discovery is and how attorney-client privilege works, but it is important you teach them, guide them, and keep guiding them. The easiest way to describe privilege is to tell them that if this or that issue went to court and a lawyer wasn't cc'd on the email or the message wasn't marked "attorney notes," "attorney-client privilege," or "confidential," their emails would be allowed to be read by the judge, jury, and other side. This can sometimes even include text, Slack, and Teams messages, so they should know to be careful what they put in writing and, if it needs to be in writing, to mark it confidential and include counsel.

I've found the best way to get the business to cooperate with cautionary communications is to encourage people to cc an in-house lawyer whenever there is something they think could result in a dispute or lawsuit or whenever they're told to cc a lawyer and then, if they can remember, to try to put "confidential" in the subject line of the email. I also let them know if I mark an email "confidential," "attorney-client privilege," or "attorney notes" along with "do not forward," they should keep me cc'd and not forward it—if they need to add folks, they can cc them. I also want to make sure they're aware that marking something confidential or sending it to a lawyer doesn't guarantee it will be protected from being shared with outside parties, but it helps.

Restoring Relationships

Despite best efforts, proactive approaches, and responsive and timely reviews of deals and asks, the legal department and in-house counsel will have issues with various people and departments. Whether one lawyer, one businessperson, or the deal volume (or lack thereof) is the root of the issue , it is important to get the legal and nonlegal teams back to being communicative and cooperative.

One way to do this is to have top-down reminders from execs of the value all departments bring and what will and won't be tolerated. The blame game truly is a waste of time, but it happens. If the top can let the ranks and departments know they need to get together and reset, it will happen.

Another way to restore relationships is a retroactive check-in. If things start getting finger-pointy, you've got to fix it. Start with the goal: good deals done in a timely manner, mitigating unreasonable risk, and amplifying good deals. Then ask: What are we doing right or wrong, and how can we fix it? How do you view us or the deals? Take that information away, and then follow up and let them know your thoughts as to what is going right, what is going wrong, how they can fix it, and how you view them or the deals, with the reminder that the goal is to get the team back to working with each other.

Proactive debriefs are great. Before things are going wrong, send an email about why a deal went smoothly or why there were some speedbumps and how to avoid them in the future. Ask what others thought.

Actually, what are pretty worthwhile are socials and a humane touch. On the social front: Let everyone do a social gathering (even a virtual one) so they see and are reminded that despite work and emails, we're all people, and largely decent, with hobbies, family, and friends, and we should try to take that humane understanding back to deals. Remember to check in once in a while on the personal side of stuff after such socials. On the humane front: Try to remember to thank folks, to wish them happy holidays, and to be empathetic.

Lastly and importantly, remember, there are boundaries and respect levels that need to be maintained. If someone is simply difficult and no tactic is working, and if any lines of professionalism, including untrue accusations or lies, are crossed, your boss, HR, and their boss need to know what will and won't work for future interactions with such a person. In my experience the people who are overly difficult to work with just really aren't great at their job—everyone knows it—and they're not very nice and resentful of those who are kind, care, and do well. Even if they are good at their job (rare, and post investigations often show some cut corners to act badly and do well), it is rare that the amount of toxic and antagonistic baggage that a performer (but bad egg) brings in is not worth the short- or long-term consequences they create. If that person is not retrained and is allowed to continue with such behavior, then perhaps someone other than you can work with them. Try that—if not, it may be time to look somewhere else if that person has power. Which leads me to Part 3: Maintaining the Role.

PART 3: CLOSING OUT THE IN-HOUSE COUNSEL 101: MAINTAINING THE IN-HOUSE COUNSEL ROLE

The in-house counsel gig, to me, is great, but it can be very frustrating. The tactics above make it less frustrating, but since new folks are always being hired, new deals are always coming in, and old deals are always getting messy, it is a constant challenge. To maintain the role, remember: It is a marathon, not a sprint. Also, you'll need to know about the corporate country club and what a GC job might be like down the road, but before that, remember these key points.

Department Dynamics

In-house counsel—at least to be happy and successful in it—is not really a job where you can fly under the radar, sit in your office, research and draft, and come and go as you please. You are highly visible and needed by many different people and departments, which to me is an honor and privilege but can be demanding. You are working with the business every day, so to maintain the role, it is really helpful not only for the other departments to understand who you are, how you work, what you need, and what you do, but also very important for you to understand each department—their pressures, goals, styles, and the main people you'll work with in those departments. Direct and honest conversations are critical. Here is my experience so far with each department and their dynamics with legal so you can get ahead of what will likely occur to make for smoother interactions and better, faster work quality for all.

Sales and Marketing
The pressure for sales is they have to keep bringing customers in, get them to sign contracts and pay, make sure everyone is happy and making money, and repeat that more and more each quarter. They have numbers they have to hit, and if they don't, they suffer financial or job consequences. It is a tough job that requires many spinning wheels. The in-house counsel helps them with their contracts to formalize their deals. Without the contract, there really isn't a deal yet. Sales gets frustrated with legal when contracts take longer than they want. They need to have a reasonable understanding of the average time to ink a deal and be made aware up front and throughout as to why things are taking long. If they are smart and sophisticated, they will offer to step in and help motivate the other side, show up to meetings, and answer your questions thoroughly. An unso-

phisticated, less experienced, or selfish salesperson will bring half-baked ideas but never see them through. Raise these folks up to a level where you're both on the same team, working together to get good deals done.

Marketing has to pitch the company, product, and service. They only have a certain budget, they need to get the word out with relatively little language/time allowed, and they have numbers they have to hit, or they suffer financial and job consequences. They need legal to review their contracts for marketing contractors and review their pitches and slogans to add terms and conditions. They most often get frustrated with legal if they have to change what they're saying, and they're emotionally committed to it—even little tweaks can frustrate them. The fact of the matter, though, is that if what they're saying isn't true, your company could be sued, and any money made from that campaign plus multiples more could be lost in a lawsuit because of an illegal, unlawful, or misleading ad. In-house counsel should be able to get marketing as close as it can to the original razzle-dazzle marketing campaign they wanted and try to keep the terms and conditions as tight as possible. The terms and conditions are usually longer the vaguer the marketing campaign is.

Finance and Accounting
This department has more of a support function to the business, like legal. Many in this group have worked with in-house counsel before. Where they are math minded, lawyers are strategy

and risk minded, and the pair is actually quite nice together. In my experience finance and accounting are great for working through contract issues, settlements, etc., with. This department feels similar pressure to the legal department from sales and marketing, who need finance and accounting to pull off what they need to pull off.

Customer Service

Like finance and accounting, the customer service team works well with legal. They're trying to triage issues to settle and solve them. Legal and customer service departments that work well together often avoid or quickly settle regulatory or litigation issues. The customer service team handles not only consumers but sometimes commercial customers. It is not an easy job. The customer service team is relying on sales and marketing to be truthful to customers because if the customer feels misled, they become very demanding and hostile to customer service. A smart customer service team is careful about what they say and confers with legal on the front end for bigger issues. This team should be advised that if there is a lawyer involved or threatened to be involved, they should raise the issue with in-house counsel.

Compliance

This department is often above the legal department or within it. Like finance, the compliance team supports the business similarly to legal. The pressures it has are the same as finance, accounting, and legal. This team is usually easy to work with because they've worked with in-house counsel before and their role is similar.

Engineering and Operations
This group is not only math minded but they're systems and processes minded. They often get frustrated and confused as to how people create unreasonable gaps in and interpretations of contracts, make assumptions, and are hostile and demanding for reasons they can't comprehend. Things for this group tend to be white or black. They neither understand nor want to be a part of ambiguity. They often have not worked with legal before and are hesitant to make statements they're not 100 percent positive about. They need to be advised that legal is not trying to trap them, that their feedback—even if it is qualified with "it depends"—is critical for the in-house counsel to deal with issues. Lastly, even if they don't think something will result in a lawsuit or customer service issue if it happens in the field, they need to escalate what happened whenever a customer or vendor has caused an issue.

Executive Team
This group works with lawyers all the time. Sometimes they don't understand the difference between an in-house lawyer and law-firm lawyer. A law-firm lawyer has much more time to draft and think through an issue, way more resources to dig in and provide almost-perfect answers, and usually multiple people (associates and paralegals) helping them. The executive

team wants you to be direct. They get frustrated when legal only brings problems. To work best with them, keep emails short, have quick calls, and, if you don't know something, as mentioned before, say it; don't try to hide it, but do say you'll find out and follow up. Also remember: your job is to inform them, but they may decide not to take your advice. As long as they are aware of the impact, as execs, that is their call to make. If they are deciding to do something illegal or unlawful (which is different than risky), then you should figure out with your state's bar and ethics committee what may need to be done.

Stay Informed

For the in-house counsel role, stay informed in your company's area of business, service, and/or products. Take CLEs that are relevant to your job or your company. Subscribe to blogs of law firms that specialize in your area of law or industry. I really like Practical Law for resources (however, it is expensive) and Box for organization (make sure it's secure). Be the value-add for the knowledge you have. Read, listen, and pay attention to outside counsel's advice. Be decent with opposing counsel. Finger-pointing is not a smart tactic on this marathon where relationships matter, and most in-house lawyers do change companies here and there. Some jurisdictions require you to register as in-house counsel, and you must maintain your license as active in most places. Be friendly and professional with the business. There is a balance between being yourself and being a robot. The business needs to know you're human but also needs to be confident you know what you're talking about—or at least will find out. I also recommend you do some reading about business and management and motivation/morale. As in-house counsel, you're more business facing than law facing if you're not in a specialist role. I like *The Monk and the Riddle*; *Relentless*; *Creativity, Inc.*; *Built, Not Born*; *Drive*; *The Happiness Advantage*; *The Slight Edge*; *As a Man Thinketh*; and *The Goal*.

Pro Tips (as Promised)

I very much recommend releases if there is ever a settlement. I am a fan of severance packages with firings (and releases). Be careful sharing your personal phone number, and ideally, get two phones (for discovery reasons). Don't worry about being overly responsive because it will create some expectation of continued rapid response; just simply respond with, "Usually this would take three to five days, but I was able to get to it ASAP today." Do make sure you respond at least to say, "Received," so the business isn't in the dark. I do recommend two monitors and a solid chair for hours on end of sitting. Be careful about being in too many meetings—you need time to work. When it comes to litigation, really do let the business know the time and money it may take to win there. Lastly, professional plaintiffs are tough, but a good, effective law firm with the right micromanagement can get it sorted quickly. Class actions are not a joke, so make sure to monitor marketing and sales. Form contracts are clutch if you can get the business to try very hard to use them with only a few exceptions.

As far as the corporate country club and a GC role, remember, we all have responsibilities. Inside most companies, politics is real. People finger point, people hire friends from other jobs, and people hire family. People are insecure and posture. People are people. Sometimes those people find similar career-driven or power-inclined people or even hobby sharers and start getting exclusive. The corporate country club is the group that has the most power and can make your life difficult or easy depending on if you are a friend of the club, member of the club, or enemy. Do your best to be a friend. Membership can come with strings that in-house counsel has to be wary of. An enemy of the club with power is dangerous, and pressure put on other execs that you're difficult or incompetent, even if likely untrue, can impact your day to day. The best way to stay friends with the club is to be responsive. Let them know why you're doing what and by when, and remind them that you'll make it happen if you can but that you have to do your job. The ultimate decision isn't with you, anyway, just the job of informing whoever it is with. Membership in and friendship with the corporate country club does come with perks—as they move upward within a company or move to another company, so, too, can you—but you've got to remember your ethics, duties, and ultimate responsibility are to the company, not necessarily any particular person or group within the company.

At some point you may be or have been invited into a GC

role. Is the GC role worth it? I have held semi-GC roles. At this point with two young kids, having worked directly for and having been a pseudo-GC, I can say it is a lot of work. You're basically on call full time for executives. You've got to manage lawyers and nonlawyers; multiple departments usually roll up to you; and you have to manage execs, manage legal issues, schmooze with big vendors and customers, appease the board, and play therapist and mediator between other execs, all while also being an in-house counsel. It often pays well, but it is very time consuming. Make sure the package is worth the commitment (and potential headache).

Each department should take the attitude when hiring that they're the gatekeeper, and whoever they bring in can change the dynamic of the culture and deals. If everyone is bringing people on with the right intent and makes sure they jibe to a reasonable level, work will be sustainable. If you can find a way to jibe, you'll be more valuable.

It is really important to raise the business and individuals up because truly, many have not worked with in-house counsel before, and if they know how to do it right, their life, your life, and the business all benefit.

Snapshot of a Successful In-House Counsel and Legal Department

The successful in-house counsel will have forms he or she can send to the business to use for almost any occasion or quickly tweak for the needed person. The business will enjoy going to the in-house counsel in appropriate situations on the front end and see the in-house counsel as a teammate and value-add. The business will schedule meetings and send asks in a way that allows the in-house counsel to best support and respond. The business will use NDAs, be cautious about what they put in writing, and understand what is and isn't urgent. The business will know what the contract review policy is and understand how long most things take. The business will understand basic legal concepts. The in-house counsel's boss can trust that the in-house counsel does their job well, treats other departments well, makes reasonable decisions, and provides reasonable guidance in a timely manner with the facts and within the limited time that they have. The legal department is not viewed as a cost center, enjoys one another's company, and learns from one another, and most are happy where they are. Outside counsel spending is low. Communication and collaboration are frequent, and legal is adding value.

So with that being said, do your best to add value as in-house counsel. Raise other people up. Communicate, cooperate, and enjoy the in-house counsel role. Remember, you can and should draw respectful lines and create fair and reasonable boundaries and ways of working that work for you. As in-house counsel, a lot of folks will need your guidance, and that is great, but don't let the perception of power go to your head or use the role in a political or abusive way. We all usually end up bumping into people outside of work and often switch companies, so add value and be decent, and expect the same from those you work with. As I mentioned, I am a resource if you want help.

Conclusion

I'll leave you with four pieces of wisdom as an in-house counsel:
1. Do the best you can with the time you are given.
2. When it comes to relationships and politics, if you won't be worried about the issue five years from now, don't spend more than twenty minutes worrying about it now.
3. If most days you can look at yourself in the mirror at the end of the day and think, I earned my paycheck and did my best today, you're on the right track.
4. If you're doing the right thing, but the business doesn't respect your lines or your guidance and it's a toxic place, start job hunting and networking; sophisticated companies are always looking for good in-house lawyers.

I very much love the in-house role. It is not for all lawyers. If you give it a try or are in it, I hope this book helps. As I mentioned in the introduction of the book, I offer three products to make your in-house life easier.

Good luck! Add value! Thrive! Remember to reiterate that legal does not want to kill deals or even slow them down; we want to make sure the business truly understands the deals, and the deals are as profitable as possible and free of unreasonable risks—in short, that the opportunity is worth more than the cost, both short and long term.

ABOUT THE AUTHOR

The author is from Boston. He has lived across the United States and in a few European countries. The author started working at eight years old at a famous bar in Boston that his father managed. The author went to Xaverian Brothers Highschool. He earned degrees in business and politics from the University of Connecticut as an honors scholar. He also earned a law degree from Tulane Law with a focus on transactions and international law. He studied law in Germany at Bucerius Law. The author worked almost full time while in college and law school. The author also clerked at a law firm in New Orleans, worked for the government with security clearance, and now consults with and works for global corporations. The author has two daughters and an awesome wife that he met in law school. When not working or parenting the author is reading, oil painting, traveling, or attempting some new hobby. He hopes you enjoy this book.

www.ingramcontent.com/pod-product-compliance
Lightning Source LLC
Chambersburg PA
CBHW070246220526
45465CB00004B/1539